THE KIDS'

HORSE

BOOK

Owl Books are published by
Greey de Pencier Books Inc., P.O. Box 53,
370 King Street West, Suite 300, Toronto,
Ontario M5V 1J9

Distributed in the United States by Firefly
(U.S.) Inc., 230 Fifth Ave., Suite 1607,
New York, NY 10001

This book was published with the generous
support of the Canada Council and the
Ontario Arts Council.

Cataloguing in Publication Data

Funston, Sylvia
    The kids' horse book

ISBN 1-895688-07-8

1. Horses – Juvenile literature. I. Title.

SF283.F86 1993   j636.1   C93-093649-3

Cover concept: Wycliffe Smith
Cover design: Word & Image Design Studio
Front cover photo: ©Kendra Bond
Back cover photo: ©Clix Photography
Text design and art direction: Word & Image
Design Studio

Printed in Hong Kong

E F G H

THE KIDS'
HORSE
BOOK

Written by Sylvia Funston

OWL

Greey de Pencier Books

Contents

Welcome to the World of Horses

One day, several years ago, my family fell in love with horses. Well, with one horse in particular. Better make that a pony. Bubble Up was her name. She was the most sweet-tempered, gentle-natured pony that we had ever met. She was bright, inquisitive and my, how she loved to jump and show off in front of a crowd!

Bubble Up was our daily companion for almost three years before we had to move back into the city and find her another comfy, country home with plenty of horses for company and another family to love her to pieces. The goodbyes went on for days.

It's been many years since we parted, but no one in my family has ever lost the sense of wonder over the strong bond that formed between us and that pony. If this book helps you to understand why horses are such special animals and why people are able to form such lasting friendships with them, I'll be happy. And I'm sure Bubble Up would be, too.

Sylvia Funston

Bubble Up with her good friend Sara Funston

Why Are Horses So Special?

Because they are graceful.
Because they are intelligent.
Because they are beautiful animals.
And because they are gentle and kind.
These are a few reasons I like horses.

◀ *Jenny Thornhill, age 9*

Patsy has been a special pony. I like her spikey mane and forelock. This is a picture of me when I first learned to ride her.

Marion Andrew, age 9

I've been riding since I was five. This is my pony Shadow. I had lots of fun helping my dad "break" him to saddle.

Jennifer Robson, age 12

Ernie is a special horse. He listens to my stories, he never gets mad, even when I ride badly, and he likes my hugs.

Ainsley Hayes, age 11

8

I love going to my
Uncle Mark and
Auntie Amy's farm. I
get to feed the horses.
Painted Native loves
carrots.

Joshua Cherun, age 10

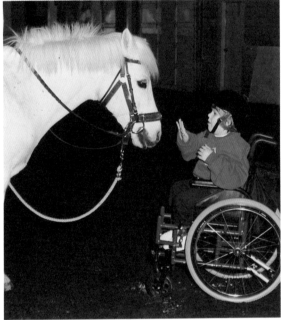

I like horse-back riding at C.A.R.D.
(Community Association for Riding for
the Disabled). Hrimmer and the other
horses are friendly.

Adrienne Martino, age 7

Riding my Aunt Caren's
horse Jonathan is fun, but
I like Shetland ponies best.
They're so small and cute.

Leslie Raichle, age 14

Where Do Horses Come From?

Whatever it was that killed the dinosaurs 65 million years ago, it had no effect on the small, otter-like mammals called *Condylarthra*. In fact, with the dinosaurs out of the way, *Condylarthra* flourished. From this humble little mammal came all the world's hoofed animals, including horses.

On these pages you'll find five stages in the development of the horse. They start with a fox-size descendant of *Condylarthra* that padded around on dog-like feet, and they end with the ancestor of today's horses, zebras and donkeys. Can you place the stages in the right order by matching up each statement with its correct picture?

Answers on page 72

How to Measure a Horse

The height of a horse is taken from the top of its shoulder—its withers—down to the ground. The measurement is given in "hands high" (hh). One hand equals 10 cm (4 inches), the average width of an adult's clenched fist. A pony that measures 10 hh, or 10 fists placed one on top of the other, stands 100 cm (40 inches) tall at the shoulder.

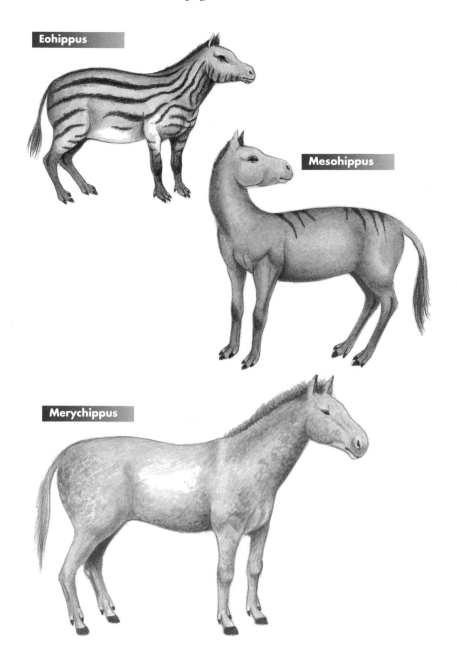

Eohippus

Mesohippus

Merychippus

Pliohippus

Equus

1 My padded front feet have four hoofed toes, but my back feet have only three. I chew leaves, berries and fruit with my three grinding teeth, and stand just over 3 hh.

2 Look closely at my three toes: the middle one has a hoof but the two side toes have become useless dew claws. My strong teeth chew grass, and I stand almost 9 hh.

3 I'm the ancestor of today's horses, donkeys and zebras. I look like a modern Przewalski's horse. I have strong teeth for chewing grass, and I stand over 13 hh at the shoulder.

4 I am the first horse ancestor to have only one hoofed toe on each foot, making me faster than *Merychippus*. I eat grass, and I stand just over 11 hh.

5 Can you see three hoofed toes on both my front and back feet? I eat leaves, berries and fruit with three more grinding teeth than *Eohippus*, and I stand 5 hh.

Did You Know?

Ancestors of the horse went through three important changes that helped them to survive.
- Their feet grew smaller, rounder and tougher so that running on hard ground didn't hurt them.
- Their legs grew longer, making horses faster runners than most of their enemies.
- Their teeth and jaw muscles grew stronger and bigger so that they could chomp on grass all day long.

The Horse Up Close

The horse's long neck lets it graze easily without having to bend its legs— allowing wild horses to flee instantly if danger approaches.

Ears that can swivel 180 degrees like radar dishes can hear just about anything that catches the horse's attention.

Big eyes, set high up and to the side of its head, give the horse almost wrap-around vision.

As the tops of the horse's teeth get worn down from constant chewing, the teeth grow in some more from underneath, like your fingernails.

The horse's large teeth with their long gripping edge are the perfect shape for cutting and pulling up grass.

The horse has extra-large nostrils to take in huge snorts of air because it cannot breathe through its mouth.

Those flaring nostrils have been known to sniff out a horse's home from several kilometres away.

When a horse runs fast its muscles gobble up oxygen. Inside that huge chest is a large heart and lungs that provide plenty of oxygen when needed.

A horse can run fast over rough ground without sprains or twisted joints because its legs only move forwards and back, not from side to side.

Long, well-spaced legs cover plenty of ground with each stride.

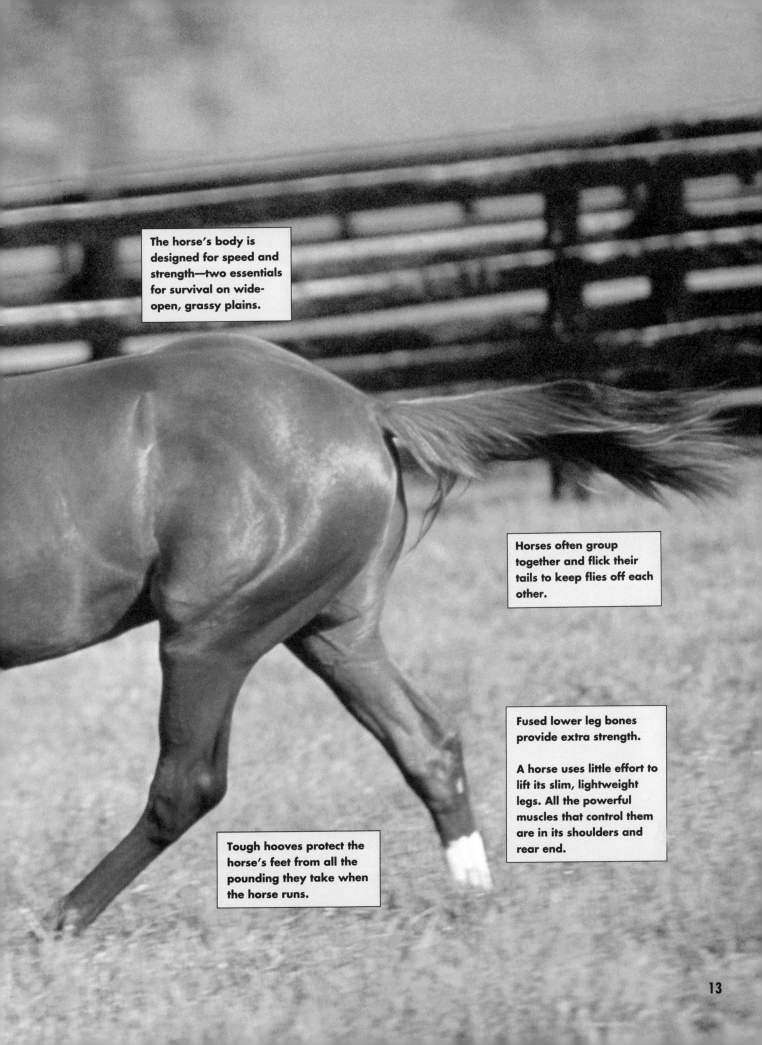

The horse's body is designed for speed and strength—two essentials for survival on wide-open, grassy plains.

Horses often group together and flick their tails to keep flies off each other.

Fused lower leg bones provide extra strength.

A horse uses little effort to lift its slim, lightweight legs. All the powerful muscles that control them are in its shoulders and rear end.

Tough hooves protect the horse's feet from all the pounding they take when the horse runs.

13

Horse Family Tree

Wild Horse (present day)

Wild Ass (present day)

M any kinds of horses have come and gone since leaf-eating *Eohippus* first appeared 52 million years ago. When grasslands began to spread millions of years later, one kind of horse switched from eating leaves to eating grass. And it's just as well! If it hadn't, horses would have been as extinct as the dinosaurs. None of the leaf-eating horses survived.

Equus
(2 mya)
Ancestor of the wild horse, the zebra and the wild ass crosses into Asia and South America but dies out in North America after the Ice Age.

Pliohippus
(15 mya)
Speed increases as single-toed hoof evolves.

Horses with one toe branch off here.

Merychippus
(17 mya)
Grasslands spread. Bones fuse in leg for greater strength. Teeth grow stronger.

Horses that eat grass branch off here.

Mesohippus
(32 mya)
As the ground gets firmer, legs get longer, teeth get stronger.

Epihippus
(38 mya)
As leaves get tougher, more chewing teeth grow.

Eohippus
(52 mya)
No grass. Lives on swampy ground. Eats leaves, berries and fruit.

Condylarthra
(65 mya)

Legend:
Leaf-eating horses - ✤
Grass-eating horses - ⩔
mya - million years ago

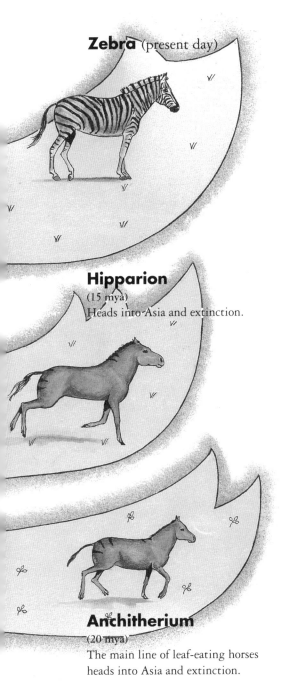

Zebra (present day)

Hipparion
(15 mya)
Heads into Asia and extinction.

Anchitherium
(20 mya)
The main line of leaf-eating horses heads into Asia and extinction.

Tapir

Rhinoceros

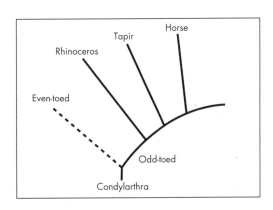

A few horse relatives

The fox-size *Condylarthra* is the ancestor of many hoofed animals. Some of them, including pigs, cows, antelopes, giraffes and aardvarks, have an even number of toes. Others have an odd number of toes. Horses, rhinoceroses and tapirs belong to this odd-toed group of animals, as this "family bush" shows.

Oldies but Goodies

Although some people think that all modern horses evolved from one type of horse, others think that they had at least three different ancestors. By today's standards, all of these horse ancestors are considered ponies because they all stood less than 14.2 hh.

Steppe Horse of Asia

This big-headed horse with its upright brush of a mane and a short, strong body probably had zebra markings on its legs and shoulders and a donkey-stripe down its back. Today, its features can be seen in the Przewalski's horse, the wild horse of the Gobi Desert in Mongolia.

Steppe, Forest and Plateau ancestors of today's horses.

Forest Horse of Europe

Heavier and slower than the Steppe, the Forest horse, with its short, strong legs and broad, rounded hooves, is thought to be the ancestor of today's work horses. Its thick coat might have been spotted or striped so that the horse could blend in with the dappled shadows of its forest home. The Forest horse was usually found in cold, wet climates.

Plateau Horse of Eastern Europe

With its lighter body and long, slender legs, it is likely that the Plateau horse is the ancestor of today's lightweight ponies and finer-built horses. It lived in the warmer parts of Asia and northern Africa. Today, its features can be seen in the Tarpan, a breed that officially became extinct at the end of the last century but which has been revived by breeding Tarpan-like horses.

Modern descendants of the Steppe, Forest and Plateau horse.

Did You Know?

During the Old Stone Age, over 3 million years ago, many types of horses roamed Europe. They left behind their fossilized bones and, in some cases, their pictures. On cave walls and roofs throughout France can be found paintings of Exmoor, Fell and New Forest ponies, and even a fat Clydesdale look-alike.

A Baby Is Born

Most wild foals are born in the spring so that they can grow fat and sleek before they face their first winter. When they reach their first birthday, male foals are called colts and females are called fillies.

The mother of this foal waited 11 months for this moment. Her baby's two front feet enter the world first, followed quickly by its head and the rest of its body. The foal is born in a skin-like bag which splits open as the baby emerges from its mother's body or shortly afterwards.

Quickly, the mother begins licking her baby. The strong action of her tongue stimulates the flow of blood through her baby's body, peels off the skin-like bag and dries the little foal's coat. The licking also reassures the foal and allows the mother to become familiar with her baby's scent.

The still-damp foal wobbles to its feet and searches for its mother's nipples to get its first drink of milk.

By the time the foal is one month old, it will have doubled its birth weight. It will spend the long summer days playing with other foals and running to its mother for drinks of milk.

After struggling to reach up for its first taste of milk, this newborn is content to settle down for a well-earned nap, safe in the knowledge that its mother is close by.

Wild Horses

Wild eyes and long flashing manes, the thunder of hooves in a cloud of swirling dust—these are the images of a herd of wild horses fleeing from danger. When a herd feels threatened, the head mare leads the other mares and young horses to safety, while the stallion brings up the rear, ready to fight off any attackers. It's the same all over the world...

Mustangs

Mustang

Believe it or not, until European explorers brought their horses with them to North America, a horse hadn't galloped across its plains for thousands of years. Horses became extinct in North America at the end of the last Ice Age. Today's mustang herds which live in the mountainous west and midwest states are descended from horses that escaped from European explorers and several plains tribes. In 1971 a law was passed to protect mustangs.

Dülmen

Since 1850, Germany's only herd of native ponies has been owned by the Duke of Croy. The Dülmen herd lives wild in woodlands and moorlands set aside especially for them by the Duke. Each autumn, however, yearlings (one-year-old ponies) are rounded up and auctioned after being branded with the Duke's coat of arms. The rest of the herd is set free to return to the wild.

Dülmen

Przewalski's Horse

The wild horse of the Mongolian steppes, named after Colonel Przewalski who discovered it, is the only horse that has lived completely free of contact with people. All other wild horses live free because they were able to escape from people a long time ago. Because the Przewalski has never been tamed, it has a wild animal's natural fear of people and can be skittish and aggressive in captivity. The Przewalski is endangered, so several zoos are breeding them to save them from extinction.

Sable Island Horses

Sable Island is a small, windswept, sandy island off the coast of Nova Scotia. Thousands of sea birds and seals live there. Surprisingly, so does a herd of horses. How they got there is a mystery. But any horse that can survive Sable Island's winter blizzards and a diet of tough marram grass deserves the special law that the Canadian government passed in 1961 forbidding anyone to interfere with them.

Wild Ponies of the British Isles

Nine types of wild ponies live in remote parts of the British Isles: Exmoor, Dartmoor, New Forest, Dales and Fell in England; Welsh Mountain ponies in Wales; Shetland and Highland ponies in Scotland and Connemara ponies in Ireland. Like the Icelandic ponies of Iceland and the Haflinger ponies of Austria, they all make excellent riding ponies once broken in. (You can see all of these ponies on page 32.)

Tarpan

The last wild Tarpan was killed in 1879 in Russia, and the last captive Tarpan died in 1887. How then, can there be a wild herd of Tarpans still living in Poland? Upon the death of the last Tarpan, the Polish government collected several Tarpan-like horses from farms and turned them loose in two protected forests. The breeding experiment was successful; today's Tarpans look very similar to the wild Tarpans of the 1870s.

Brumby

Australia is one of the few places in the world that the horse never reached during its evolution. All the sturdy brumbies that live in the mountains of Queensland, New South Wales and Victoria are descendants of ponies that early settlers brought with them from the island of Timor off the northeast coast of Australia.

Camargue

The beautiful gray horses of the Camargue live on the marshy lands at the mouth of the Rhône River in France. After 2,000 years of living on such soft land, their feet have grown bigger and their hooves have flattened, distributing their weight more evenly. Camargue foals are born black. Only after several years do they grow the distinctive gray coats of their herd.

The next time you visit a stable, ask a rider to show you a horse's frog. Don't worry — this frog won't leap away! It's a shock-absorbing wedge of horn in the center of each hoof. For more unusual horse facts, try your hand at these questions.

Answers on page 72

1▶ What should you do to show you're friendly when you meet a horse for the first time?
a. Offer to shake hands.
b. Blow gently up its nose.
c. Cross your eyes and smile.

2▶ You're helping someone to saddle a horse English-style and you're asked to pass a numnah. What is it?
a. a soft pad that goes under the saddle
b. a delicious horse treat
c. a metal bit that goes in the horse's mouth

WHERE DOES A HO

3▶ A horse's height is measured in hands. One hand equals 10 cm (4 inches). How many hands high (hh) must a horse measure to qualify as a horse and not as a pony?
a. 13.2 hh
b. 14.2 hh
c. 15.2 hh

4▶ You're horseback riding and you come across a hog's back. What would you do?
a. Ride away before the hog turns around.
b. Get off the horse and walk — it's a low bridge.
c. Jump it — it's a type of show-jumping fence.

5 ►What should you comb with a curry comb?
a. Nothing on a horse—use it to clean hair out of your horse's body brush.
b. a horse's whiskers
c. a horse's eyelashes

6 ►In which event at a rodeo do cowboys and cowgirls compete against each other?
a. a pie-throwing contest
b. barrel racing
c. square-dancing

7 ►Who do you call when your horse needs new horseshoes?
a. a harrier
b. a farrier
c. a furrier

10 ►If you're using coconut shells to make a sound like a galloping horse, which rhythm should you use?
a. clip clop clip clop, clip clop clip clop
b. clip clip, clop clop, clip clip, clop clop
c. clip clop clip, clip clop clip, clip clop clip

11 ►Where is a horse's elbow?

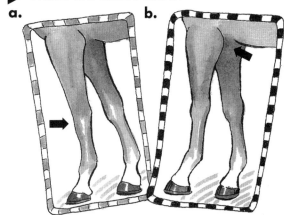

SE HIDE FOUR FROGS?

8 ►You should always tie up a horse with a quick-release knot. Which of these two knots releases when you pull the end of the rope?

9 ►What would you be planning to do if you put a doughnut on your horse's coronets?
a. Jump over fences.
b. Give your horse a bath.
c. Give your horse its dinner.

12 ►You're a dressage* rider and you ask your horse to do the piaffe. What do you expect your horse to do?
a. Spin in a circle.
b. Trot on the spot.
c. Bow its head.

13 ►How many faults do a horse and rider collect for a knockdown in a Grand Prix show-jumping event?
a. one fault
b. two faults
c. four faults

14 ►A hippologist is someone who studies:
a. horses
b. hips
c. hippos

15 ►Where would you find a fork, a skirt and a horn?
a. on the inside of a barn door
b. on a western saddle
c. on the front of a stagecoach

*   Dressage is the very disciplined, fancy stepping some horses are trained to do.

Top 20 Horse Parade

O ut of more than 200 breeds of horses, 3 stand out because they have played such an important role in the breeding and development of many of today's superb horses. Unlike most other breeds, which are each bred in one particular country, the Arab, the Barb and the British Thoroughbred are bred all over the world.

▲ Arab
14.2 – 15.1 hh

Originally bred in the Arabian peninsula

This spirited, beautiful and gentle horse is so swift that it earned the title "Drinker of the Wind" from the Bedouin tribes of the Arabian deserts. Renowned for its hardiness and strength, the Arab is a champion over long distances. Between 1689 and 1728, three Arab stallions established the bloodlines for the British Thoroughbred.

▼ Barb
14 – 15 hh

Originally bred in Algeria and Morocco (the Barbary Coast)

More than 1,000 years ago, Barb horses carried Moorish invaders into Spain. There, the Barbs bred with Spanish horses to produce Spain's famous Andalusian horses. Later, Barbs were taken north to England where they were bred with British racehorses to improve their speed and stamina. It took 500 years for the British Thoroughbred to be recognized as a breed.

Akhal Teke
14.2 – 15.2 hh

(Turkoman Steppes, Russia)

This tough, strong-willed horse has a long history as a battle horse and can survive extreme desert conditions. Its coat is often the color of burnished gold.

American Quarter Horse
15.2 – 16.1 hh

(United States of America)

Named for the quarter-mile races it regularly won in the 18th century, the Quarter Horse—part Thoroughbred, part Mustang—is a terrific pony for cowboys.

◄ British Thoroughbred
14.2 – 17.2 hh

Originally bred in England

Also known as the racehorse, the British Thoroughbred is the fastest horse in the world. It is also one of the finest riding horses, although its fiery nature makes it a horse for experienced riders only. The Thoroughbred has the courage and stamina needed to be a champion in many equestrian sports. Through interbreeding, the Thoroughbred has improved many other breeds of horses and ponies in countries throughout the world.

American Saddlebred
15 – 16 hh

(United States of America)

This graceful horse with its unusual high-speed prancing gait became famous for carrying many well-known generals during the American Civil War.

American Standardbred
15.2 – 16 hh
(United States of America)

The world's best-known trotter takes its name from the one-mile (1.6 km) standard time that all harness racers have to meet at a speed trial before they can enter a race.

Andalusian
About 16 hh
(Spain)

This Spanish descendant of the Barb is a strong, active horse that combines agility and fire with a gentle nature. Look for its flying mane and high-stepping action.

Appaloosa
14.2 – 15.2 hh
(United States of America)

Named for Washington State's Palouse Valley, this strong, intelligent horse has six patterns of spots: frost, leopard, snowflake, marble, spotted blanket and white blanket.

Cleveland Bay
16 – 16.2 hh
(England)

The stamina, speed and endurance of the "Yorkshire Coach Horse"—boosted by Thoroughbred blood—help this powerful bay to excel in the show ring.

Canadian Cutting Horse
15.2 – 16.1 hh
(Canada)

This intelligent horse has a natural talent for cutting a cow away from the rest of the herd. Its powerful hind quarters allow it to turn quickly and jump from a standstill to a gallop in an instant.

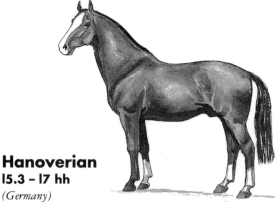

Friesian
About 15 hh
(Netherlands)

The "cheerful" Friesian has been a popular saddle horse, trotter and farm horse. Three Dutch farmers saved it from extinction before World War I.

Hanoverian
15.3 – 17 hh
(Germany)

When you come across an intelligent horse with powerful muscles and a great sense of balance, chances are it's a Hanoverian. It's probably a terrific jumper, too.

Lipizzaner
15 – 16 hh

(Austria)

Intelligent, sweet-natured Lipizzaner stallions train for seven years in medieval war maneuvers—the basis of today's dressage—before performing at the famous Spanish Riding School of Vienna.

Morgan
14 – 15.2 hh

(United States of America)

Today's strong, good-natured Morgans are descended from a horse that was named for its owner: Justin Morgan. The original horse was famous for its strength in log-pulling contests and its speed in quarter-mile races.

Paso Fino
About 14.3 hh

(Puerto Rico)

A descendant of Spanish horses, this intelligent, good-tempered horse is named for the way it walks. Paso fino is the term to describe a very comfortable four-beat gait.

Percheron
15.2 – 17 hh

(France)

The Percheron's elegance probably comes from its Arabian blood. Percherons are bred all over the world, but the French consider true Percherons to be only those that are bred in the Perche region of France.

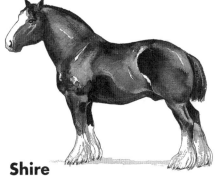

Shire
About 17 hh

(England)

The tallest of all horse breeds, the gentle Shire is descended from the Great Horse that carried knights into battle. It also has Thoroughbred ancestors.

Tennessee Walking Horse
15 – 16 hh

(United States of America)

This good-tempered, comfortable riding horse was bred by Tennessee plantation owners. It was known as the "Turn Row" because it could walk between the rows of crops without damaging them.

Waler
About 16 hh

(Australia)

Brought to Australia by settlers, the brave, sensible Waler is a Spanish/ English cross. A monument in Sydney commemorates the 120,000 Walers that served during World War I.

Popular Ponies

Ponies are horses that grow no taller than 14.2 hh, and some of them are much smaller...

Avelignese
13.3 – 14.2 hh
(Italy)
The kindly, hardy Avelignese can pick its way over high mountain trails in the worst winter conditions. It is also strong enough to work on farms.

Connemara
13 – 14 hh
(Ireland)
For as long as people can remember, Connemaras have run wild in the mountains of the west coast of Ireland. This easygoing pony does best when it grazes on poor pasture.

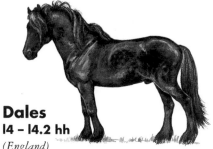

Dales
14 – 14.2 hh
(England)
The powerful Dales pony is sensible, quiet and sure-footed. The Dales has helped farmers for centuries and has even worked as a pack pony in lead mines.

Dartmoor
Up to 12.2 hh
(England)
A close relative of the Exmoor, the kind, sensible Dartmoor makes an ideal first pony. It also has a reputation as a natural jumper.

Exmoor
11.2 – 12.3 hh
(England)
You can recognize the strong, intelligent Exmoor by its unmistakable heavy-lidded "toad" eyes and its thick tail with a fan-like growth at the top.

Falabella
Under 7 hh
(Argentina)
No bigger than a large dog, the friendly, intelligent Falabella is too small for riding, but it makes a great family pet or harness pony.

Fell
13 – 14 hh
(England)
At one time, the Fell pony carried 100 kg (220 lbs) of lead each day from lead mines to the coast, 50 km (30 miles) away. Today, it is a well-loved riding pony.

Fjord
13 – 14.2 hh
(Norway)
This charming pony with a brush-like mane is a sure-footed work pony in mountainous areas. It has changed little since the days when it was a Viking fighting horse.

Galiceño
12 – 13.2 hh
(Mexico)
Ancestors of this highly intelligent, gentle, ranch pony might have been among the 16 horses that landed on the American mainland when Cortes invaded Mexico.

Gotland
12 – 12.2 hh
(Sweden)
This hardy, sometimes obstinate, Scandinavian pony dates back to Stone-Age times and is valued by both farmers and trotting fans.

Haflinger
Up to 14.2 hh
(Austria)

This strong, sure-footed mountain pony is a cross between the Arabian and the draught horse, and its docile behavior makes it an ideal first pony for a new rider.

Highland
12.2 – 14.2 hh
(Scotland)

The sensitive Highland pony is the biggest and strongest of all the British pony breeds. Once a work horse, today the Highland is popular as a family pony as well as for trekking.

Icelandic
12 – 13 hh, occasionally bigger
(Iceland)

If you borrow a friendly, but independent, Icelandic pony from a friend and ride it a great distance, be sure to tether it securely when you stop or it will turn around and head for home.

Konik
about 13.1 hh
(Poland)

The Konik combines the toughness of its ancient Tarpan relatives with a kind nature and a willingness to learn. Its Arabian blood makes it look more like a small horse than a pony.

Mongolian
12 – 13.2 hh
(Mongolia)

Bred for centuries by nomadic tribes for herding and riding and as pack ponies, these tough little ponies survive on whatever they can find.

New Forest
12 – 14.2 hh
(England)

This friendly, quick-to-learn pony is a mixture of many breeds—Clydesdale, Arab and Thoroughbred among them. It never gets upset by traffic and is one of the safest ponies for children to ride.

Pony of the Americas
11.2 - 13 hh
(United States of America)

This small Appaloosa was first bred in 1956 by crossing a Shetland stallion with an Appaloosa mare. It is a versatile, gentle and willing pony.

Shetland
Averages 9.3 hh
(smallest ever – 6.2 hh)
(Northern Scotland)

Immensely strong for its size, the gentle, courageous Shetland has worked on farms and in coal mines. It has lived on the Shetland Islands for 2,500 years.

Welsh Mountain
Up to 12 hh
(Wales)

This good-looking, popular pony has roamed the mountains of Wales since Roman times. Its Arab qualities probably come from two Arab stallions that once ran wild in the Welsh hills.

Welsh
12 - 13.2 hh
(Wales)

A one-time sheepherding pony, the Welsh pony is now *the* riding pony of all the Welsh breeds. The largest Welsh ponies are developed by breeding with Arabs and Thoroughbreds.

Big and Small, Old and Tall

Because people have been breeding horses for so long, they've had time to develop breeds with special abilities or looks, such as the tiny Falabella and the mighty Clydesdale. Besides dogs, how many other animals can you think of that range in size from miniature to very large?

Smallest Breed

The miniature Falabella takes first prize for being small enough to walk under your kitchen table.

Tallest Horse

Although the Shire, at 17 hh, is the tallest breed, a Percheron cross called Firpon obviously didn't know this. He didn't stop growing until he was so tall that his ears would almost have reached the top of a city bus.

Oldest Breed

The Arab is thought to be the world's oldest, purest horse breed.

Oldest Horse

Many domestic horses have been known to live well into their 30s. An English barge horse called Old Billy earned his name by the time he died in 1822—at the age of 62.

Heaviest Horse

If you put a Belgian stallion named Brooklyn Supreme on one side of a set of scales, you'd need one-and-a-half subcompact cars on the other side to balance him.

Driest Horse

An Akhal Teke is reported to have crossed 1500 km (900 miles) of desert without so much as a sip of water.

World's First Jockeys

A novel form of horse racing made its debut at the 648 BC Olympic Games in Greece. Each horse had a rider instead of being allowed to run free. Obviously, the idea caught on!

JUMP OFF!

A show-jumping board game for two to four players

Rules

1. Use one die. Use coins or buttons as playing pieces.
2. The high roll starts the game.
3. Follow the numbered squares from start to finish.
4. Follow the instructions on each square you land on.
5. You must roll the exact number to finish.
6. The first player to finish wins the game.

START

1

2 Knockdown! 4 faults. Back to start.

3 You clear crossed poles. Move ahead 2 squares.

4

5

6 Horse rushes triple bar. Go back 2 squares.

7 Horse is jumping smoothly. Roll again.

8

9 You clear water combination jump. Move up to 15.

10 You miss pole-over-hayrack jump. 4 faults! Go back to 4.

11 Great jump over parallel oxer. Move ahead number rolled.

12

13

14 First refusal at wall. 3 faults! Go back 6 squares.

15

16

43

44 Horse slips on tight turn. Go back 5 squares.

45

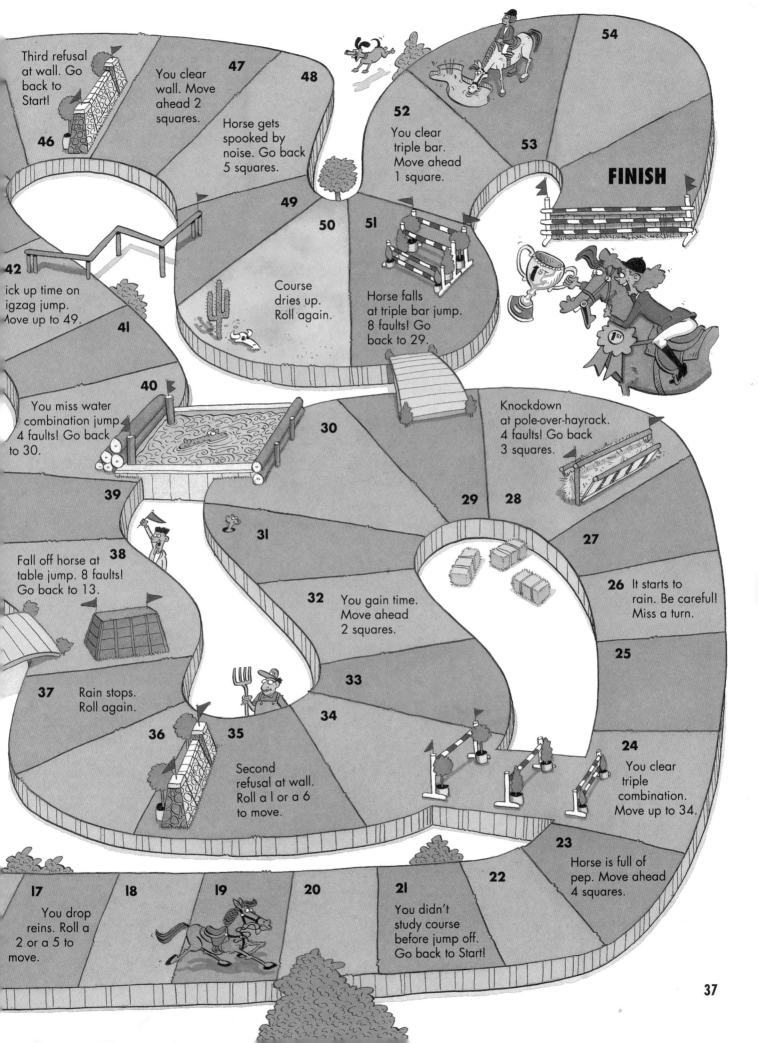

46 Third refusal at wall. Go back to Start!

47 You clear wall. Move ahead 2 squares.

48 Horse gets spooked by noise. Go back 5 squares.

49

50 Course dries up. Roll again.

51 Horse falls at triple bar jump. 8 faults! Go back to 29.

52 You clear triple bar. Move ahead 1 square.

53

54

FINISH

42 ...ick up time on ...igzag jump. ...ove up to 49.

41

40 You miss water combination jump 4 faults! Go back to 30.

39

38 Fall off horse at table jump. 8 faults! Go back to 13.

37 Rain stops. Roll again.

36

35 Second refusal at wall. Roll a 1 or a 6 to move.

34

33

32 You gain time. Move ahead 2 squares.

31

30

29

28 Knockdown at pole-over-hayrack. 4 faults! Go back 3 squares.

27

26 It starts to rain. Be careful! Miss a turn.

25

24 You clear triple combination. Move up to 34.

23 Horse is full of pep. Move ahead 4 squares.

22

21 You didn't study course before jump off. Go back to Start!

20

19

18

17 You drop reins. Roll a 2 or a 5 to move.

HOW TO DRAW A HORSE

If you can draw a square, a triangle, a circle and a rectangle, you can draw a horse. To find out how, follow this easy, step-by-step guide.

1 ▶ Draw a square.

2 ▶ Divide it in two. The horse's body fits in the top section. Its legs fit in the bottom one.

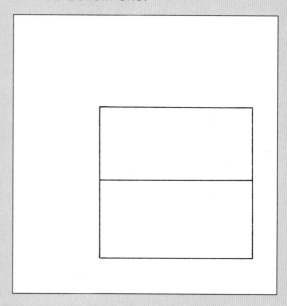

3 ▶ Draw two long triangles from the top left corner of the square. Erase the ends of the triangles as shown here.

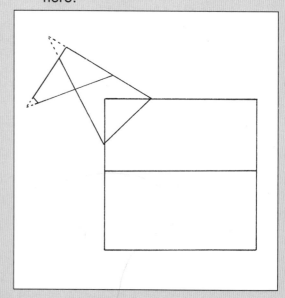

4 Block out where the legs will go by drawing a rectangle for the front legs and an uneven rectangle for the back legs.

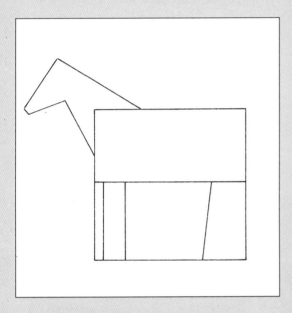

5 Add two circles—one for the shoulder and one for the hip.

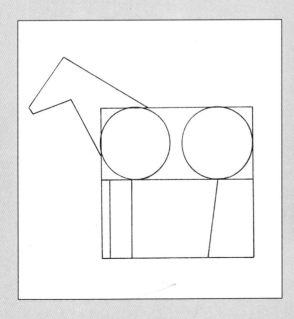

6 Using the lightly penciled shapes as a guide, draw the outline of a horse.

7 To complete your drawing, erase the light pencil lines. Then add details and shading like this:

Where Would We Be without Horses?

Without people, the horse would not have developed into the animal it is today. And without horses, the world would be a very different place.

Battle Horses

As long ago as 1000 BC, Chinese officers were commanding their battles from horse-drawn chariots. The use of horses in war times led to the development of better roads and faster communication and changed the course of history for many nations. For instance, Julius Caesar's first invasion of Britain failed miserably, but he succeeded on his second attempt in 54 BC, largely because his forces included 2,000 soldiers on horseback.

Great Horses

It's impossible to think of Britain during the Middle Ages without thinking of knights on horseback. A knight in full armor weighed as much as two heavyweight wrestlers. The Great Horse of England, thought to be an ancestor of today's Shire, was the only breed that could carry this much weight into battle. Yet, if William the Conquerer had not invaded England in 1066, there might never have been any knights to protect the weak or fight the Crusades. Why? Because he brought with him from France a cavalry of heavy horses, and from them England's Great Horse was bred.

Fast Horses

With the invention of firearms in Europe, a horse on the battlefield had to be fast and light on its feet. This was the type of horse that the Spanish explorers took to North America and which dramatically changed the lives of several tribes of native peoples. Even though there had not been any horses in North America for thousands of years, plains and prairie tribes quickly became expert riders. For the next 300 years, they hunted buffalo on horseback, hitched horses to their sled-like travois to haul their belongings from one camp to the next, and raced and fought on horseback. The Comanches, in particular, were such skilled riders that in the midst of battle they could drop out of sight over one side of their horses and fire their arrows from under their horses' necks.

Barge Horses

In towns and cities, horses hauled goods. In Europe, goods were often moved on barges along networks of canals, and these barges moved by horsepower. Barge horses were intelligent, strong and agile. Pulling ropes that were attached to the barge, they walked along the land at the sides of the canal, jumping over any gates in their way on the tow-paths. They could even cross from one side of the canal to the other by jumping on and off barges.

Mail Horses

As roads improved, lighter and faster horses were used to pull coaches and carriages. Communication sped up as mail was carried by horse-drawn mail coaches. The most famous mail service of all time, however, did away with coaches to gain extra speed. The United States' celebrated Pony Express ran from 1860 to 1862 from Missouri to California. Four hundred ponies were kept saddled up and raring to go at relay posts along the 3200 km (2,000 mile) route. Riders galloped the ponies from post to post, covering a tenth of the total journey each day. Without horses, communication across a continent the size of North America would have been almost impossible before the invention of the telegraph.

Work Horses

When heavy horses were no longer needed in battle, they took over from oxen working in the fields. They pulled farmers' ploughs and carried produce to market. Today, you can still see horses doing farm work in some European countries.

Carriage Horses

In the early 1500s, the roads were in such poor condition that heavy horses were needed to haul wagons and coaches. Queen Elizabeth I once took a journey from London to Warwick, England in a large state wagon drawn by six huge horses. She couldn't sit down for a week afterwards! It was not unusual to see as many as 400 heavy horses pulling her wagon trains when she visited far-flung regions of her realm.

Pit Ponies

As factories sprang up all over Europe, horses were needed more than ever to move heavy goods. In Britain, ponies were put to work in the coal mines, where they continued to work until the 1970s.

Cow Ponies

In Australia and North America, horses made the great cattle ranches possible. The heyday of the cowboy in North America began right after the American Civil War and lasted until the beginning of this century. Today, in parts of North America, cowboys still round up cattle on horseback and drive them to market because it's less expensive to use horses than to pay fuel and freight charges on the road or the railway. And besides, it's a lot more fun.

Dancer's Scrapbook

Dancer became one of the lead horses in the Royal Canadian Mounted Police's famous Musical Ride when she was five years old. If Dancer had been able to keep a scrapbook during her two years of training, here's what it might have looked like:

Here I am, a scrawny little filly. Who would think that I'd get chosen to learn how to be a fancy stepping horse in the world's most famous musical ride?

Dominic and Daisy are being nosy. My trainer has just discovered that I opened the door to the oat room last night and helped myself to a midnight snack. Now I'm in trouble!

This is my trainer. I finally allowed him to put a saddle on me today and I didn't buck once. It was a good game while it lasted.

I've been here six months now and do a lot of this. Working on the lunge line is supposed to help me even up my stride. Sometimes there are lots of distractions while I'm working, but I try to ignore them.

Just after this photo was taken, Dominic nipped me during our dressage lesson. I waited until he passed by again and gave him a swift kick to his rear end. My trainer laughed so hard he almost fell off.

Well, I finally made it into the Musical Ride. This is everyone's favorite part. Don't we look great?

I hate saying goodbye, but my trainer has a new three-year-old to get into shape, and I'm on my way to Osaka in Japan with the Musical Ride. This is the life for me!

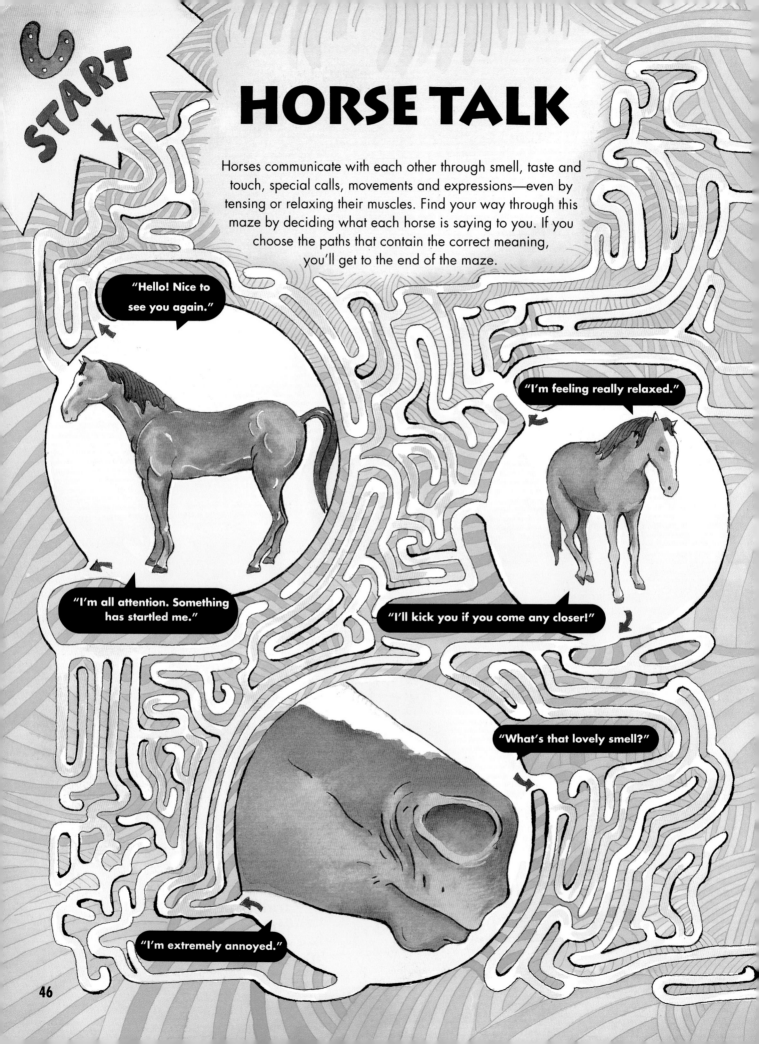

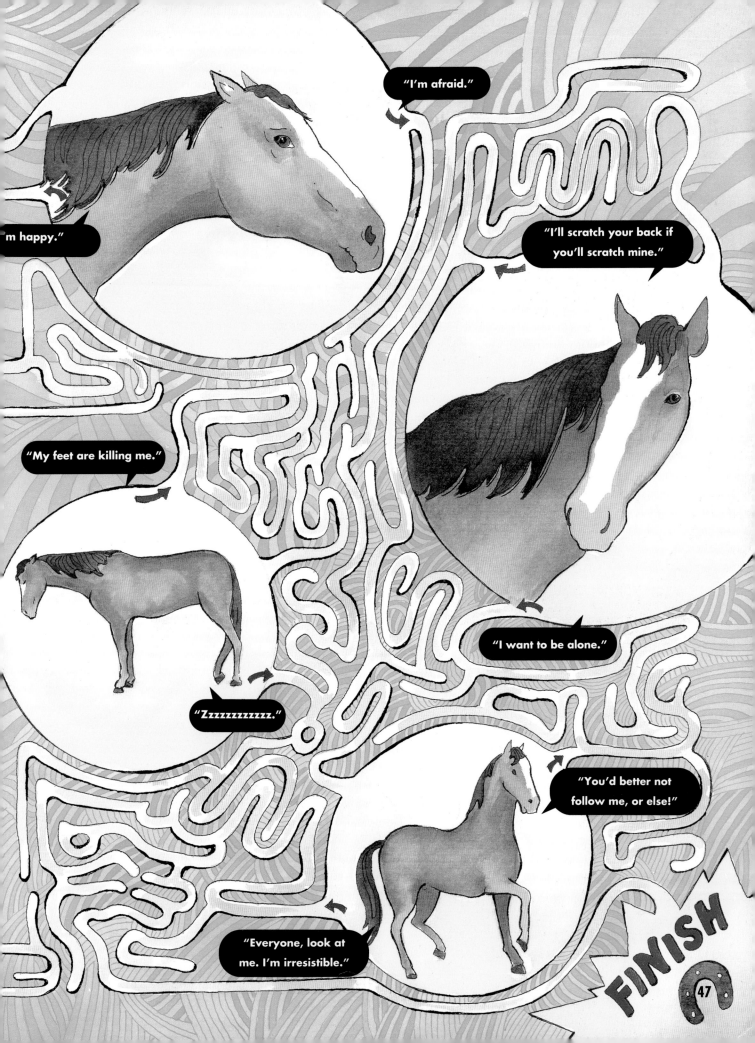

Horse Sense

A Story by Lucy Rees

The horse galloped madly around the pen, his head turned to the outside as he searched for an opening. But there was none. The smooth, high bars encircled him inescapably. In the center of the circle was the man. The horse knew that men were hunters. They trapped him in corners, caught him and drove him into small, dark spaces that rattled terrifyingly. They put ropes on his head and tied him up. He had learned that fighting the ropes was pointless. Even when the men touched him, he did not fight, though he hated their touch. Beneath his skin, the muscles were tight with tension, and the sensation was alarming. Now,

without a rope to restrain him, he put as great a distance as possible between himself and the man.

After a while, his panic died down and he settled into a steadier gallop, still with his head turned to the outside. But he could glimpse that the man was no longer standing, but was walking in a small circle, keeping level with his shoulder as he galloped. This was a sinister development; the horse straightened his head so that he could see better, and he cocked an ear at the man.

"Thanks," said the man. "Decided to pay me some attention, eh?"

It was easier galloping with his head straight, and the horse could now see that the man was quite

relaxed. He did not have the tense, predatory look of a stalking wolf, nor the jerky movements of a frightened horse; rather, he looked more like a sleepy mare watching her foal. The horse slackened his pace, swung his neck down to ease the tension in it, and relaxed his tail. The man stepped back into the center of the circle, and seemed almost to go to sleep. Feeling the pressure of his nearness reduced, the horse slowed to a trot. When the man resumed his slow circling, the horse sprang into a gallop, but soon slowed again. When the man stepped back, he trotted, stretching his neck to the ground. It felt good.

As they worked on in this way, the horse's alarms became briefer, his paces slower, until eventually he dropped to a walk. Finally, when the man stepped back, the horse stopped and wheeled to face him, blowing down his nostrils as a warning.

"Oh, okay," said the man, and squatted on his heels. The horse watched him intently. He had never really examined a man: whenever they had been near before he had been too busy looking for an escape route. So he peered, leaning forward to catch a whiff of scent, listening to the man's quiet muttering. When he had finished his scrutiny, he rocked his weight back, relaxed one hip and waited. The man stood up and moved slowly towards him. When he was a couple of paces away, the horse's nerve broke. He wheeled and galloped away.

"If you want to leave, I'll help you," said the man, waving him forward gently. But this time it took fewer repeats before the horse calmed and stopped. When the man came forward, he left a good three paces between them, watching the horse shrink back onto his heels. He stepped back again. The horse straightened. The man turned and walked away. The horse leaned forward, watching him. The man walked towards the horse again until he pulled back, then stopped and turned away. Back and forth their bodies went, like a pair of dancers connected by an invisible bond, a bond that grew stronger each time it was tested. But when the man reached out a hand, the horse shook his head and shied away.

Within 10 minutes, the horse understood all the moves of this game, for it was the same game that he played with his herd-mates. When the man flicked his hand, as an irritated horse flicks his tail, the horse moved away. When he dropped his

shoulders and stood still, the horse stopped. The man knew how close he could approach, then he would turn, drop one shoulder and half glance behind him, as a mare watches the foal following her. And the horse followed. Three paces apart, they walked round the ring, stopping and starting in unison. Suddenly, the man bent down. The horse found his nose above the man's shoulder, smelling him, smelling his hair, feeling his ear, feeling the man shake with laughter at the tickling whiskers. The man waited until the horse had finished, then he stood up slowly. They stood almost touching each other for a full minute. Then the man put his hand on the horse's shoulder and began to scratch, as one horse nuzzles another when they have decided to be friends. The horse felt good. At last, he was safe.

It's in a horse's nature to get along well with other horses. When two horses groom each other by scratching and nibbling at their manes, withers or rumps they are saying, "You are my special friend." Some domestic horses tell their owners that they are special friends by scratching their owners' backs while they are being brushed.

When Is a White Horse Not a White Horse?

When it's a gray! A horse that has white hair but dark skin is called a gray. Only if it has white hair and pink skin is it a truly white horse — but then it's called an albino. Now that you know the difference between a genuine white horse and a horse that merely looks white, test your powers of observation on horses of other colors. Can you match up each horse with the correct description of its color?

Black

Brown

Bay

Chestnut or Sorrel

Gray

Did You Know?

A horse's "points" refer to the tips of its ears, its muzzle, mane, tail and lower legs. A horse is said to have black points if all of these areas are black.

Dun

Cream

Roan

Piebald or Pinto

Palomino

Skewbald or Pinto

1 I'm a bright mahogany color, but all my points are distinctly black.

2 I can range in color from almost white to iron gray. If my coat is covered with little, dark specks, I'm called flea-bitten.

3 My color can range from fiery ginger to dark red. Usually my points are the same color, but occasionally my mane and tail are flaxen.

4 Look for a horse with large black and white patches and that's me. If my face is mostly white, my eyes are often blue.

5 I, too, have a dramatic coat, but its patches are white and bay or chestnut. My eyes are often blue.

6 I can be the color of a mouse or creamy butter, or I can be shimmering silver with black points. I often have a list—a black line—down my back.

7 Sometimes I'm such a dark brown that I look almost black. My points are always brown.

8 My color is known as strawberry because my coat is a mix of white and chestnut hairs. When it's a mix of white and black, I'm called a blue, and when it's white and bay, I'm known as a red.

9 I'm black all over, except when I have white markings on my face or legs.

10 My coat is the color of a new, gold coin and my mane and tail are gleaming white.

11 Beneath my pale cream coat you'll find pink skin. If my eyes are blue—known as wall eyes—I'm called a cremello.

Answers on page 72

Bits and Pieces

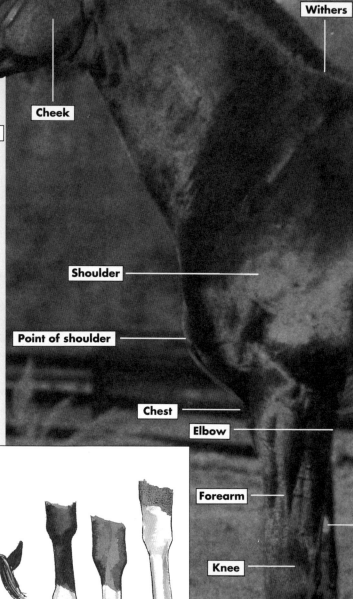

Poll

Forelock

Crest

Withers

Nostril

Cheek

Muzzle

Chin

Shoulder

Point of shoulder

Chest

Elbow

Forearm

Knee

Cannon

Hoof

T he next time someone asks you where your horse keeps its chestnuts, you don't have to smile weakly and say, "Um...er...in its pocket?" Check out what all a horse's bits and pieces are called. Then you can point knowingly to the hard knobs high up on the inside of a horse's legs and say, "The chestnuts are right there, where else?"

Stars, snips and stripes

All those little white marks on horses' faces and legs have special names. Look at the heads and legs below to find out what those names are.

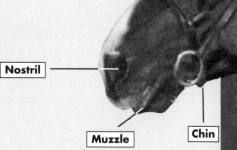

Star

Blaze

Snip

Stripe

White face

Sock

Stocking

Leg

Did You Know?

The hard chestnuts high up on the inside of a horse's legs are what is left of its "thumbs." Each chestnut is grooved, producing a "thumbprint" that is unique to each horse.

Point of hip

Loins

Back

Croup

Dock

Thigh

Gaskin

Stifle

Chestnut

Hock

Pastern

Coronet

NICKER SNICKERS

What well-known phrase and activity is hidden here?

Horsing around

What runs all around the paddock but never moves?

A fence

It has four legs, eats hay, has a tail and sees just as well from either end. What is it?

A horse with its eyes shut

What do you find at the front of an elephant but at the back of a horse?

The letter "e"

What do you call a pony with a sore throat?

A little hoarse

What is as big as a horse but weighs nothing at all?

A horse's shadow

What is a foal after it's four days old?

Five days old

How far can a horse run into the woods?

Half way—after that, it's running out of the woods.

What kind of horse can jump higher than a house?

All kinds—houses can't jump.

What side of a horse has the most hair?

The outside

A cowboy rode into town on January 5th, stayed in town for a week and rode out again on January 5th. How is this possible?

January 5th is the name of his horse.

Why are horses such bad dancers?

Because they have two left feet.

What goes clip, clop, clip, squish?

A horse wearing one wet sneaker

55

Tack Box Tangle

Uh-oh! Someone knocked over a tack box and its contents got mixed up with several things that horses don't need. Can you figure out which grooming tools belong in the tack box?

Answers and explanation of tools on page 72

Saddle Up!

Both English and Western saddles were developed from long-ago war saddles, which were designed to give riders a secure, comfortable seat no matter how long they were on horseback. Western-style saddles still look a little like those used by ancient warriors. English-style saddles have been streamlined for hunting, jumping and playing polo.

Western-style Riding

Cowboys spent many hours each day in the saddle. They needed saddles that wouldn't let them slide around and give them or their horses saddle sores. So they adapted the deep Spanish saddles that the Conquistadors brought to the Americas.

One type of early cowboy saddle had two sets of cinches to hold it firmly in place so that the rider wouldn't be unseated by a steer that was attached to it by a rope. Its deep seat helped a tired rider stay on his horse, and its steel horn and fork were strong enough to take the strain caused by roping cattle. The saddle's wide skirt spread the rider's weight evenly over a large area of the horse's back, making it easy on the horse over long distances.

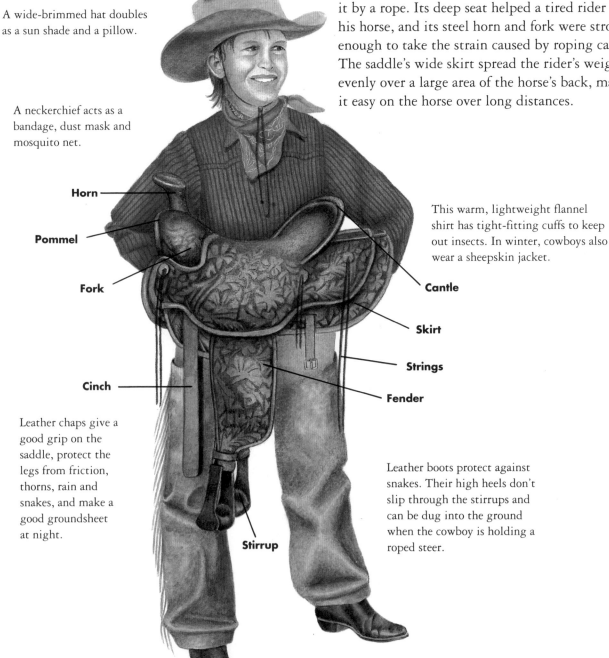

A wide-brimmed hat doubles as a sun shade and a pillow.

A neckerchief acts as a bandage, dust mask and mosquito net.

This warm, lightweight flannel shirt has tight-fitting cuffs to keep out insects. In winter, cowboys also wear a sheepskin jacket.

Horn

Pommel

Fork

Cantle

Skirt

Strings

Cinch

Fender

Leather chaps give a good grip on the saddle, protect the legs from friction, thorns, rain and snakes, and make a good groundsheet at night.

Leather boots protect against snakes. Their high heels don't slip through the stirrups and can be dug into the ground when the cowboy is holding a roped steer.

Stirrup

English-style Riding

A large pommel can be painful for the rider when the horse jumps, so it's no wonder that it has practically disappeared from the English saddle. Because sport riding requires good balance from both horse and rider, the stirrups are shortened and set forward so that the rider's weight moves forward, directly over the horse's center of gravity.

The streamlined shape of the English saddle allows the rider to be in close contact with the horse. Even the small, metal stirrups are designed to turn the rider's knees in to get a better grip on the horse, and their treads slope down towards the horse's rear to help keep the rider's heels down for better balance.

The hard hat with a safety harness protects the rider's head during falls from the horse.

A cotton shirt is cool in summer and absorbs perspiration without being bulky.

A riding jacket fits closely so that it doesn't flap around and catch the wind—or worse, a branch or a fence.

Cantle

Waist

Pommel

Panel (Lining)

Skirt

Stirrup leather keeper

Girth

Jodhpurs are formfitting, stretchy trousers with leather pads on the inside of the knees to increase the rider's grip on the saddle.

Saddle flap

Stirrup leather

Long hunting boots fit over jodhpurs to protect the rider's legs from branches and thorns during the hunt. Their heels prevent the feet from sliding through the stirrups and their smooth soles allow the boots to be pulled free of the stirrups if the rider falls.

Going Riding

Ears
They should be alert and usually carried forward. A pony that often lays its ears back may be bad-tempered.

Neck
For good balance, the neck should be longer on top than underneath.

Eye
A pony with big, kind-looking eyes usually has a gentle nature.

The first time you mount a pony you'll probably be so excited you won't care what it looks like. But the more you ride, the more you'll realize that some ponies give a more comfortable ride than others. Here's how to recognize a smooth-riding, great-looking pony when you see one.

Chest
A pony with a broad, deep chest will have staying power.

Would you choose this pony to ride?

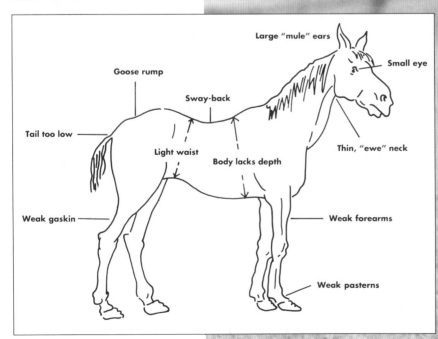

Large "mule" ears

Goose rump

Small eye

Sway-back

Tail too low

Light waist

Thin, "ewe" neck

Body lacks depth

Weak gaskin

Weak forearms

Weak pasterns

Shoulder
For smooth leg action, look for a long, sloping shoulder.

Elbow
It should move freely for easy action.

Temperament
If you ride in traffic, choose a calm pony that does not get spooked by noise.

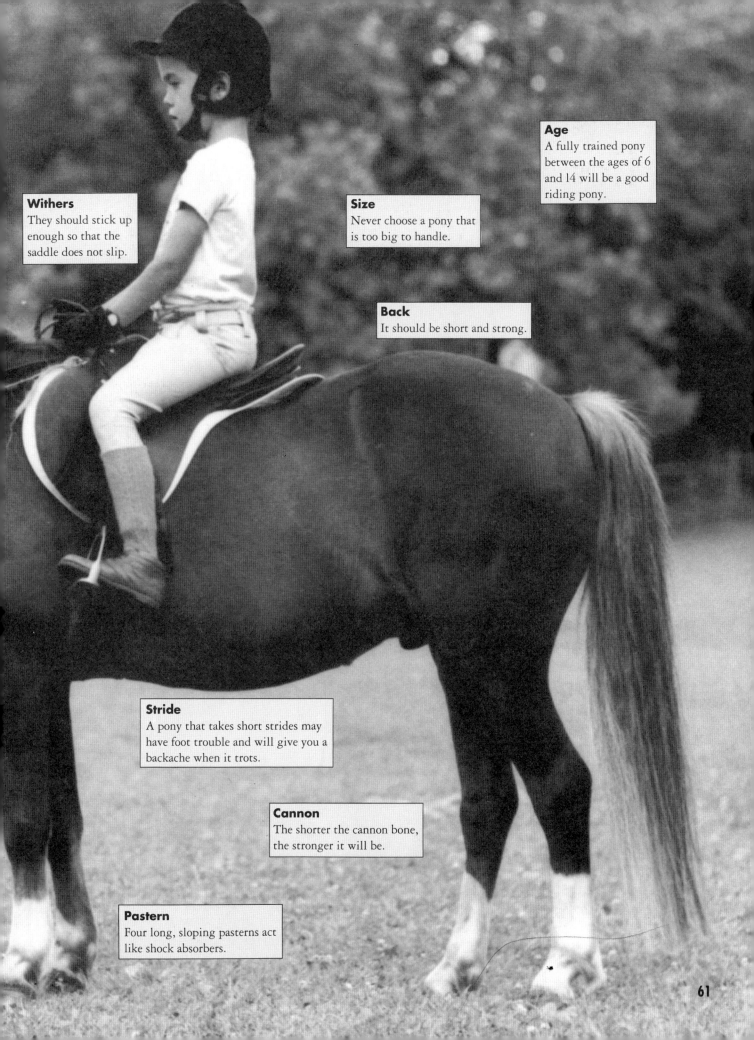

Withers
They should stick up enough so that the saddle does not slip.

Size
Never choose a pony that is too big to handle.

Age
A fully trained pony between the ages of 6 and 14 will be a good riding pony.

Back
It should be short and strong.

Stride
A pony that takes short strides may have foot trouble and will give you a backache when it trots.

Cannon
The shorter the cannon bone, the stronger it will be.

Pastern
Four long, sloping pasterns act like shock absorbers.

Giddyup!

S o you're ready to ride. On these pages you'll find a few basics to get you started in English-style riding. On the next two pages you can find out how the same thing is done Western-style.

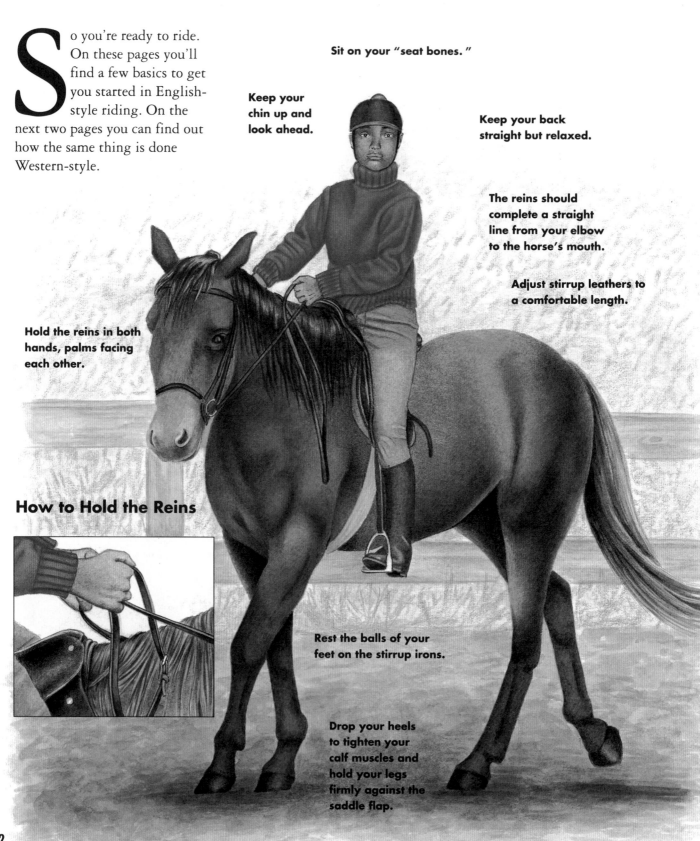

Sit on your "seat bones."

Keep your chin up and look ahead.

Keep your back straight but relaxed.

The reins should complete a straight line from your elbow to the horse's mouth.

Adjust stirrup leathers to a comfortable length.

Hold the reins in both hands, palms facing each other.

How to Hold the Reins

Rest the balls of your feet on the stirrup irons.

Drop your heels to tighten your calf muscles and hold your legs firmly against the saddle flap.

How Long Should Your Stirrup Leathers Be?

Your stirrup leathers should be as long as the distance between your fingertips and armpit. Adjust their length if necessary when you are seated on your pony.

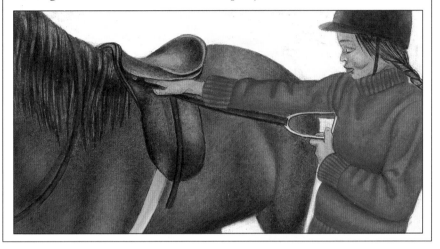

Getting Up

Always mount from the pony's left side, facing its rear.

1. Hold the pony's mane and reins in your left hand while you place your left foot in the stirrup.

2. Grab the back of the saddle with your right hand, hop lightly up and swing your right leg over the pony's back.

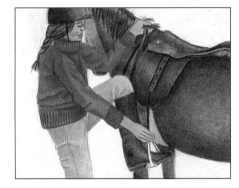

3. Sit down gently. Put your right foot in the stirrup and gather up the reins in both hands.

How to Get Your Pony to Walk

Squeeze the pony's sides with your lower legs, push down with your seat and say "Walk on" in a calm, quiet voice. As soon as the pony begins to walk, slacken the reins slightly so that your hands can move forwards and backwards with the natural rhythm of the pony's head.

How to Get Your Pony to Turn

1. Look where you want to go.
2. To turn left, hold your left leg firmly against the girth of the saddle and place your right leg behind the girth. Squeeze the left rein.
3. To turn right, reverse the leg instructions and squeeze the right rein.

How to Get Your Pony to Stop

Push your seat down into the saddle, press down with your heels, squeeze gently on both reins and say "Whoa."

Getting Down

1. Hold on to the reins and slip both feet out of the stirrups.
2. Lean forward. Place your left hand on the pony's mane, your right on the saddle and swing your right leg backwards.
3. Slide down and bend your knees before you land.

Giddyup Again!

Forget about those cowboys you've seen galloping across TV or movie screens, kicking and whipping their poor horses to get them to run faster. An expert Western rider controls his or her horse in such a relaxed, natural way that it is difficult to see that the horse is being controlled at all.

Keep your head up and your back straight, but relaxed.

Keep your shoulder, hip and the back of your heel in line. Then you and your pony will be in balance.

How to Hold Split Reins

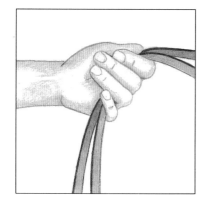

Hold the reins in one hand, just in front of the saddle horn and above the pony's mane.

Don't force your heels down too far or your lower leg will move forward. You'll move off your "seat bones" and end up behind the pony's center of gravity, which will throw you both off balance.

Getting Up

1 Stand on your pony's left side, facing its head. Gather up the reins in your left hand and put your left foot in the stirrup.

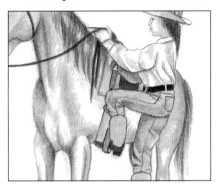

2 Grab the saddle horn with your right hand, spring lightly up and swing your right leg over the pony's back.

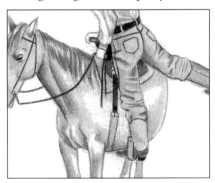

3 Stand up in both stirrups and drop your heels. Slowly bend your knees until your seat gently touches the saddle. Swivel your hips slightly until you feel that you are sitting on your "seat bones."

How to Get Your Pony to Walk

Squeeze the pony's sides with your lower legs, push down with your seat and say "Walk on" in a calm, quiet voice. Slacken the reins slightly when the pony is walking so that your hands can move with each nod of its head.

How to Get Your Pony to Turn

1 Lay the reins lightly on one side of your pony's neck and it will turn in the opposite direction.
2 Move the reins out to one side of the pony, and it will follow them with its nose.
3 Press one of your legs against the pony's side and it will turn in the opposite direction.

How to Get Your Pony to Stop

Round your lower back, put more weight on your heels and move your lower legs forward slightly. At the same time, squeeze the reins and say "Whoa."

Getting Down

This is done exactly the same way as in English-style riding.

Did You Know?

In English-style riding, the horse's gaits are called walk, trot, canter and gallop. Western-style riding has two more gaits: jog, or slow trot, and lope, or slow canter.

Amazing but True

If you live in an earthquake zone, pay close attention to your horse. It will get skittish and very noisy for no apparent reason—just before a quake.

Horses sleep for less than three hours a day and lie down for only a couple of those. In fact, lying down to rest is hard work for a horse because it has to breathe harder to help its heart pump blood around its horizontal body.

If a horse had its own way, it would eat for up to 16 hours a day. Horses' preferred foods are grasses, flowers, berries, nuts and fruits.

Horses have to be very careful not to eat poisonous foods. Why? Because special valves in their throats prevent food from coming back up. No matter how sick they feel, horses cannot vomit.

You can only focus on one thing at a time, but a horse can look at the grass it's nibbling and watch out for danger on the horizon at the same time. How? The pupils of its eyes are rectangular and can focus on two things at once.

What looks like a knee on a horse's long, strong leg is really its ankle. And don't let its lower leg fool you. It's actually part of its foot!

WHAT'S WRONG HERE?

T he people who own this paddock don't know much about looking after horses or even how to ride them. There are several things wrong in this scene. How many can you find?

Answers on page 72

68

Answers

Where Do Horses Come From? pages 10/11

Eohippus, 1 (52 mya); Mesohippus, 5 (32 mya); Merychippus, 2 (17 mya); Pliohippus, 4 (15 mya); Equus, 3 (2 mya, first true horse)

mya = million years ago

Where Does a Horse Hide Four Frogs? pages 26/27

1-b, 2-a, 3-b, 4-c, 5-a, 6-b, 7-b, 8-a, 9-a, 10-a, 11-b, 12-b, 13-c, 14-c, 15-b

When Is a White Horse Not a White Horse? pages 50/51

1-Bay, 2-Gray, 3-Chestnut or Sorrel, 4-Piebald or Pinto, 5-Skewbald or Pinto, 6-Dun, 7-Brown, 8-Roan, 9-Black, 10-Palomino, 11-Cream

Tack Box Tangle, pages 56/57

1. Dandy brush removes heavy dirt and mud.
2. Soft, body brush is used for all-over brushing.
3. Metal curry comb removes hair, dirt and grease from body brush. It is never used on a horse.
4. Rubber curry comb is used in circular motions to remove dead hair when a horse is shedding.
5. Water brush is dipped in water and used to wash a horse's feet and to dampen the mane and tail.
6. One sponge is used to clean a horse's eyes and nostrils; the other is used to clean around its tail and inside its back legs.
7. Hoof pick cleans out a horse's hooves.
8. Hoof oil is painted on a horse's hooves to keep them healthy.
9. Paintbrush is used to apply hoof oil.
10. The serrated side of a metal shedding blade is used to get rid of hair when a horse is shedding.
11. The smooth side of a metal sweat scraper is used to get rid of sweat and water when a horse is washed.
12. Mane comb is used to keep the mane and tail tidy.
13. Gentle dish detergent is used for occasional baths.
14. Hair conditioner removes tail tangles.
15. Stable rubber, or towel, is used to put a final polish on a horse's coat.

A horse doesn't need a dog collar and leash, a football, mouthwash, a toothbrush and toothpaste, a paint roller, a screw driver or a hockey puck.

What's Wrong Here? pages 68/69

1. The fence should not have been repaired with barbed wire because the animals could injure themselves on it.
2. The paddock gate should be kept shut to prevent the horses from bolting.
3. The paddock gate must have a strong lock to prevent the horses from pushing it open.
4. The horse should not be tied to a flimsy fence. If it panics, it could pull the fence down and injure itself. Instead, it should be tied to a ring on the side of the stable.
5. The horse should not be tied by its neck because it could choke. A lead shank (a strong rope with a clip on one end) should be attached to the horse's halter (a canvas or rope headgear the horse wears when not being ridden), then tied to a ring on the wall of the stable.
6. The teenager should not be using a metal curry comb on the horse. It is intended only for cleaning other brushes, and it will break the hairs in the horse's tail.
7. A horse or pony should always be mounted from its left side.
8. The pony's saddle has no cinch to keep it in place. It will slide off the pony when the child tries to mount.
9. The pony's bridle is missing reins.
10. The child is wearing shorts. To prevent chafing, jeans or long pants should be worn.
11. The dog could easily spook the pony, and the pony might throw its rider.
12. The child is wearing sneakers, which could cause problems while riding. The rider's foot could slip through the stirrup because sneakers do not have heels.
13. The floor of the stable needs a thick layer of straw. It's comfortable for the horses, and it collects horse droppings and urine, making it easier to clean the shelter each day.
14. The water trough should be cleaned out and kept filled with fresh water.
15. The foxgloves growing near the paddock gate are poisonous. The horses might eat them.
16. The pitchfork and shovel left lying on the ground are dangerous. A horse or person could step on them.
17. The wheelbarrow is missing its wheel. It is very difficult to clean out the shelter without a wheelbarrow.
18. Someone has forgotten to remove the bridle and reins from the pony that's trying to graze in the background. With a bit in its mouth, the pony won't be able to eat, and the reins could get caught on something.